Praise for the Believ

"As grandparents of 50 grandchildren, we heartily endorse the *Believe . . . and You're There* series. Parents and grandparents, gather your children around you and discover the scriptures again as they come alive in the *Believe . . . and You're There* series."

—STEPHEN AND SANDRA COVEY
Stephen Covey is the bestselling author of *7 Habits of Highly Effective People.*

"Bravo! This series is a treasure! You pray that your children will fall in love with and get lost in the scriptures just as they are discovering the wonder of reading. This series does it. Two thumbs way, way up!"

—MACK AND REBECCA WILBERG
Mack Wilberg is the Music Director of the Mormon Tabernacle Choir.

"This series is a powerful tool for helping children learn to liken the scriptures to themselves. Helping children experience the scriptural stories from their point-of-view is genius."

—ED AND PATRICIA PINEGAR
Ed Pinegar is the bestselling author of *Raising the Bar.*

"We only wish these wonderful books had been available when we were raising our own children. How we look forward to sharing them with all our grandchildren!"

—STEPHEN AND JANET ROBINSON
Stephen Robinson is the bestselling author of *Believing Christ.*

"The *Believe . . . and You're There* series taps into the popular genre of fantasy and imagination in a wonderful way. Today's children will be drawn into the reality of events described in the scriptures. Ever true to the scriptural accounts, the authors have crafted delightful stories that will surely awaken children's vivid imaginations while teaching truths that will often sound familiar."

—TRUMAN AND ANN MADSEN
Truman Madsen is the bestselling author of *Joseph Smith, the Prophet.*

"My dad and I read *At the Miracles of Jesus* together. First I'd read a chapter, and then he would. Now we're reading the next book. He says he feels the Spirit when we read. So do I."

—CASEY J., AGE 9

"My mom likes me to read before bed. I used to hate it, but the *Believe* books make reading fun and exciting. And they make you feel good inside, too."

—KADEN T., AGE 10

"Reading the *Believe* series with my tweens and my teens has been a big spiritual boost in our home—even for me! It always leaves me peaceful and more certain about what I believe."

—GLADYS A., AGE 43

"I love how Katie, Matthew, and Peter are connected to each other and to their grandma. These stories link children to their families, their ancestors, and on to the Savior. I heartily recommend them for any child, parent, or grandparent."

—ANNE S., AGE 50
Mother of ten, grandmother of nine (and counting)

When the Stone Was Rolled Away

Believe and You're There

When the Stone Was Rolled Away

Book 3

ALICE W. JOHNSON & ALLISON H. WARNER

DESERET BOOK
Salt Lake City, Utah

Library of Congress Cataloging-in-Publication Data

Johnson, Alice W.
    Believe and you're there when the stone was rolled away / Alice W. Johnson,
Allison H. Warner ; illustrated by Jerry Harston.
        p.   cm.
    ISBN 978-1-59038-723-8 3992 8147 4109
    1. Jesus Christ—Resurrection—Juvenile literature.   2. Jesus Christ—
Appearances—Juvenile literature.   3. Jesus Christ—Forty days—Juvenile litera-
ture.   I. Warner, Allison H.   II. Harston, Jerry ill.   III. Title.
    BT482.J65 2007
    232.9'7—dc22
                                                            2007005793

Printed in the United States of America
Worzalla Publishing Co., Stevens Point, WI

10   9   8   7   6   5   4   3   2   1

Believe in the wonder,
Believe if you dare,
Believe in your heart,
Just believe . . . and you're there!

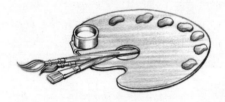

Contents

Chapter One

Easter Eggs and Birthday Cake

Grandma's annual Easter egg hunt drew family and friends from all over the county. Aunts, uncles, cousins, and many friends and neighbors who were just like family to Grandma. And by tradition, they all gathered in her backyard the Saturday before Easter.

This Easter weekend, the weather was perfect for the hunt. The morning sun filtered warmly through dozens of soft, white cottony clouds dotting a sky the color of robins' eggs. Children dashed about looking under shrubs and behind yellow tulips, and they deposited their colorful treats in their wicker Easter baskets.

Every year Katie felt certain that all the eggs had been found. Hadn't they scoured every inch of that yard? But inevitably, often many months later, one of the children would stumble onto an undiscovered treasure.

As the festivities were winding down, several of the children, their baskets laden with eggs, stood at the window of Grandma's art cottage. With their noses pressed against the glass, they strained to get a look at Grandma's creations.

"Grandma, Grandma, can we see your paintings?" they begged. (It didn't matter one bit whether you were related or not, everyone called her "Grandma," and that's the way she liked it.)

Grandma's paintings were loved by everyone. But Katie, Matthew, and their younger brother, Peter, her three grandchildren, loved them most of all. For lately, Grandma's paintings of biblical scenes had come alive for them, literally. A trip through one painting to the River Jordan, and another to the Sea of Galilee, left the children hoping desperately that the magic would continue.

No one knew the secret of their time travels, and they wanted to keep it that way. If someone found out, would the magic end? They couldn't bear the thought! So Peter got a bit nervous when all the visiting children wanted to see Grandma's work. After all, there was a brand new painting propped up on Grandma's corner easel, and Peter hoped it held another adventure for them.

"Grandma, if other kids see your new painting, will it still work?" he asked anxiously.

Grandma laughed, "What do you mean 'Will it still work'? Paintings are just for looking at, Peter. They don't have working parts, you know!"

"I know," he stammered, ". . . but . . ."

"I think we can share the painting, don't you?"

Grandma asked, with a hint of a smile in her voice and an innocent look on her face.

"Well, if . . . if you say so," Peter said, a little distressed. And off he ran to find Katie and Matthew.

The visiting children crowded at the cottage door while Grandma unlocked it and then ushered them in.

As the children milled about inside the cottage, gazing at each painting in turn, Katie and Matthew stood in the corner of the yard, watching. Peter found them there.

"Do you think the new painting will still work for us?" he asked.

"We were just wondering the same thing ourselves," Katie said.

"But could just looking change the painting?" Matthew queried.

"I hope not." Katie sounded unsure. "I don't know all the rules of magic paintings. I guess we'll just have to wait and see."

But huddled in the corner of the yard, the three children were hardly able to contain their worry.

Finally, when the last child was out of the cottage, Grandma summoned her grandchildren.

"Katie, Matthew, Peter! Everyone is ready to leave. Let's say good-bye to them, and then I have a special treat in the kitchen for just the three of you. How does that sound?"

The three excited children accompanied Grandma to the front of her house, where they tried not to look impatient for everyone to go. They hugged and smiled and waved as the other guests left, all the while wondering what surprise Grandma might have in store.

Finally, Grandma waved and shouted her last "Thanks for coming!" and ushered her grand-children into the house.

Once in the kitchen she took charge. "Everyone close your eyes!" she ordered. Opening the refrig-erator, she pulled out a double-layer German chocolate cake—her specialty! She lit the candles, turned off the kitchen lights, and set the cake on the table in front of the children.

"All right, everyone open your eyes! Let's all sing Happy Birthday!" And she began the song in her confident, but wobbly, singing voice.

"Happy birthday, to you, happy birthday, to you," the children joined her. But they didn't know whose birthday it was. So when they reached the next phrase, they stopped singing and looked to Grandma expectantly.

With gusto she sang out, "Happy birthday, dear *Grandpa*," then nodded to the children to join her, and they all sang the last rousing "Happy birthday, to you!" together.

"Let's blow out the candles together," she suggested, and on her signal they blew as hard as they could . . . and out they all went.

Grandma looked into three young faces, each full of questions. So she explained, "Today would have been Grandpa's birthday. I wanted to remember him, so we're celebrating with his very favorite cake."

"Grandma," Katie wondered, a tender look on her face, "doesn't it make you sad to think about Grandpa, with him being gone and all?"

"Well, I do miss him of course," Grandma began, "but I know that I am going to see him again one day."

"How could that be?" Peter interjected. "I thought he died!"

Grandma couldn't help chuckling, "Well, yes he did."

"Isn't that the end then?" Peter seemed confused.

Grandma slipped her arm around her youngest grandson and said, "To some people it seems like the end, Peter. But to me, it is just the beginning."

Chapter Two

Grandma's New Painting

"The beginning?" Peter questioned Grandma skeptically. "How could it be the beginning when Grandpa's life has ended?"

"He started a new life when he died, Peter, and now he's waiting for me in heaven."

Katie listened carefully to what Grandma was saying. A tear started down her cheek. "Grandma," she sniffled, "does that mean you are going to die?"

"Well, everyone has to leave the earth someday, Katie. But I think I'm going to be here for quite a little time yet." Grandma cradled Katie in the crook of her arm as she wiped her granddaughter's tear away.

"I don't want you to die, ever!" Katie declared.

"Well, when I do, I'll still be close by, watching you and waiting for you to join Grandpa and me someday. Then we'll all be together again, just like we are here," she reassured them.

"How can you be so sure about that?" Matthew had been sitting on his stool, listening intently to the conversation, trying to make sense of the whole thing.

"Matthew, you're my thinker. How I love that about you! Your mind is always working, trying to figure everything out," Grandma said to her ten-year-old grandson. "Just remember this: some things we figure out with our minds, and some things we figure out with our hearts. And in my heart, I know I will see Grandpa again. The Spirit whispers to my heart that this is true."

"Do you mean the Holy Ghost tells your heart?" Peter asked.

"Exactly!" Grandma smiled. "I know it because I feel it. Oh, children, I've been waiting for this moment all day. Who is ready to see my new painting?"

Three hands shot straight up into the air. "Well, come along then. We are going to discover some very important things together." And Grandma walked ceremoniously to the back door and stood like a sentinel as each child passed through.

Along the flagstone path and past the garden they hurried, until they were all gathered on the stoop of the charming little cottage. Guarding the doorway, Grandma pointed ceremoniously at Matthew. "Believe," she began.

"In the wonder," Matthew caught right on and finished the phrase.

"Believe," she said again, this time pointing at Katie.

"If you dare," Katie replied with a smile.

And last she pointed to Peter. "Believe," she prompted.

"In your heart," he answered.

Then she lifted her arms as if leading a choir. And on cue, they all joined together, "Just believe . . . and you're there!" Grandma stepped aside and, with a sweep of her arm, welcomed them in.

The familiar smell of oil paint greeted them. As usual, Grandma had arranged large pillows and blankets on the floor near the fireplace, right in front of the corner easel. Close by was Grandma's overstuffed rocking chair and a small table holding her large, open Bible. And right on top rested Grandma's funny little reading glasses.

Eager to experience the new painting, the children hurried to get comfortable on the pillows. Three sets of eyes inspected the unusual scene Grandma had painted this time, while behind the eyes, three minds were thinking the same thought: *Will the magic happen again?*

"All right," Grandma said, picking up the Bible. "Before we start, who knows what I've painted for you this time?"

In the center of the painting was a large rocky hill with an opening at its base. It looked a lot like a cave, but the entrance was about the size and shape of a doorway, as if it had been made by man, not nature. A great, disc-shaped rock stood at the left of the opening. And it, too, looked as if it had been carefully shaped, so it could be rolled like a tire.

Flowering vines cascaded down from the top of the stony mound. Leafy green plants and soft blankets of white blossoms filled flowerbeds in a little paved courtyard in front of the cave. A rough stone bench sat at one side in the shade of a gnarled olive tree. And through its leaves, the morning sun threw beautiful shadows over the garden scene. It was all very peaceful and serene.

In the corner of the garden, a man dressed in brown robes was kneeling among the blossoms. "Who is that man in the flowers?" Katie asked, looking at him carefully, hoping she might see him move. But the figure was completely still.

"That is the gardener," Grandma answered. "The owner of this garden, a man named Joseph, employed him to care for it."

"Is that a cave in the rock hill?" Peter asked, curious about what might be inside the dark opening.

"Sort of," answered Grandma. "What do you think, Matthew?"

"I'm not sure, but that big round stone looks like it was made to close off the doorway. So I'm going to guess that the cave was made to hold something precious," Matthew ventured.

"Good thinking," Grandma replied. "Katie, any other ideas?"

"Is that the tomb where they put Jesus after He was crucified?" Katie asked.

"Yes, Katie, you're absolutely right. This is a picture of a garden and a tomb that belonged to a man named Joseph of Arimathaea," Grandma explained.

"A tomb?" Peter asked. "What's a tomb?"

"Isn't a tomb a cave that was made to hold a dead body?" Matthew ventured. "Is that right, Grandma?"

"It is. And sometimes, a tomb is called a sepulchre," Grandma said. "You see, after Jesus died, Joseph of Arimathaea went to Pilate, the Roman ruler, and asked for the body of Jesus. When Pilate agreed, Joseph took the body down from the cross and wrapped it in linen. He owned this beautiful garden and its brand-new tomb. So he brought the body of Jesus here and laid it inside, where it would be safe."

"If Joseph wanted Jesus' body to be safe, how

come he didn't put that big rolling stone in front of the door?" Matthew wondered.

"Ah, good question, Matthew," Grandma said with an approving smile. "To answer it, I'm going to read to you from the scriptures. Everyone settle back, get comfortable, and pretend that you're there."

Grandma perched her reading glasses on the end of her nose and turned the pages of her Bible until she found the spot she was looking for. "Let's see, here we are. 'Now in the place where he was crucified there was a garden; and in the garden a new sepulchre . . .'"

Chapter Three

In the Garden

As Grandma continued to read, the children examined the painting. Was there any movement at all? Nothing!

Then Katie's attention was drawn away by the chirping of a bird. She looked out through the cottage window but couldn't seem to spot the cheerful creature. Someone poked her arm, and she turned quickly to see Matthew pointing to the painting, a wide grin spread across his face. A little bird floated against the blue sky Grandma had painted, and it landed in a flowering tree near the open tomb.

Even the gardener, kneeling among the flowers, cocked his head to listen. He stood up, stretched his tired arms, then leaned on his hoe and enjoyed the singing with a contented smile.

While the gardener relaxed, three children, half a world away and in another time, tensed with excitement, their hearts thumping loudly in their chests. Why, Peter looked as though he was going to jump right up and shout "Hooray!" But Matthew grabbed his brother's hand and pulled him close.

"Ready?" Katie whispered, grabbing hold of Peter's free hand.

"Ready!" Peter and Matthew whispered back.

"Here goes," and this time, it was Katie who reached out, pressing her finger into the painting near the large round stone next to the tomb's opening.

Whoosh! The wind rushed under and around them, lifting them up right off the cottage floor. Whoosh! With hands clasped together, all three children felt themselves being drawn into the canvas. Whoosh! And they were on their way.

"Yahoo!" Peter cried, his eyes wide with delight as his curly hair whipped in the wind.

And as suddenly as the cottage had disappeared, the three children found themselves landing in the garden Grandma had painted. "Hey, I got a new outfit," Katie exclaimed as they touched down. "This one is gray and purple, and last time it was just brown."

"Well, mine still looks like a dress," Matthew huffed, resigning himself to the fact that he was always going to end up in a tunic and sash. "But at least I'm starting to get used to it," he said with a wry smile.

"I like mine," Peter said, admiring his own brown robe, which was belted at his waist with a multi-colored scarf. "I love pretending! I only wish I had a sword in this belt."

"I'm just grateful we end up in these clothes. Otherwise, we would really have some explaining to do!" Katie rightly observed.

Just then, the nearby gardener noticed the three children standing near the entrance to the garden. "Hello! I didn't see you come in!" he said kindly as he approached them. "Have you come to see the tomb?"

"Uh, yes, I guess we have," Matthew answered hesitantly.

"It's all right, you needn't worry. Come, I will show it to you," and the gardener motioned for them to follow. At the tomb's opening, he stopped. "Here is the place where they laid the body of my Lord," he said, pointing inside.

Gingerly, the children stepped in. They were unprepared for the feelings of wonder and gratitude that overcame them as they entered the empty room, carved into the rocky hill. They stood in total silence, gazing at the stone platform where the body of Jesus had lain. Even Peter could not utter a word.

Finally, the gardener spoke, his voice subdued. "It was just above this garden, on the hill called Golgotha, that they raised a cross and crucified Jesus. My master, Joseph of Arimathaea, brought His body here to this beautiful new tomb to be buried."

"Were you here when they brought His body?" Matthew asked.

"Yes." He pointed to the stone shelf. "I saw them lay Him right here, carefully wrapped in clean linen cloth." His voice trailed off as he remembered with sadness the events of that evening. The children waited for him to continue.

"Then Romans came," he went on. "They sealed the tomb themselves with this round rock." The children followed the gardener out of the tomb and into the courtyard, where he showed them the huge stone that had been rolled in front of the entrance. "Then they posted soldiers here to guard the tomb."

Katie looked at the gardener quizzically. "Why did they have to guard Him when He was already dead?"

"Well, Jesus had prophesied that He would rise again after three days. The Romans didn't believe it was possible, but they were afraid that a believer would move the body to trick people into thinking Jesus had risen. They called Jesus a deceiver, and they said they didn't believe Him. But just to make sure, they posted the guards." The gardener couldn't help chuckling.

"Did the guards have swords?" Peter asked eagerly.

"Yes, they had swords. But those swords didn't do them a bit of good when the angels came to roll away the stone," he explained.

Peter's eyebrows shot up and his jaw dropped in astonishment. "Angels rolled the stone away?"

"Oh, yes! It was amazing," the gardener continued. "I had just left the garden when I heard a loud rumbling, and the earth began to shake under my feet. I could not imagine what was happening. I quickly ran back here to see, and I could hardly believe my eyes. The soldiers were lying on the ground as if they were dead, and the stone had been rolled from the entrance."

"Was Jesus gone?" Matthew asked.

"I was so frightened, I did not dare to look in. I thought that the Roman guards were all dead, and I did not want to be blamed. So I turned around and ran to fetch my master."

"Were the guards really dead?" Katie asked.

"No, they just looked like they were," the gardener said. "Apparently, they had fainted with fright when the angels appeared."

"So did you get in trouble?" Peter asked.

"No. When Mary Magdalene and the other women came a little later, they looked in and saw that the tomb was empty. At first, they had no idea what had happened to Jesus' body."

"They must have been sad," Katie said.

"Oh, yes, they were very sad. They loved Him so." The gardener sighed. "And so did I."

Just then, the garden gate creaked, and they all turned to see a man enter and walk to the entrance of the tomb. He peered in for a moment, and a knowing smile crossed his face.

The gardener arose and approached him. "I can tell from the look on your face that you are a believer."

"Yes, I am," the man answered. "I have come to see the place where the Lord lay."

"You have come to the right place," the gardener confirmed, "but His body is no longer

here. He is risen from the dead, just as He promised."

"Yes, I know," the man said softly, "for I have
seen Him for myself."

Chapter Four

The Empty Tomb

"Ah, you are one of the blessed people who has witnessed the risen Lord!" the gardener exclaimed. "Are you an apostle?"

"No, I am a follower named Cleopas. And you are?"

"I am the gardener here. My name is Jonas. And, oh, dear me, I have not even asked the names of my young visitors!" Jonas seemed flustered.

Katie rescued him. "My name is Katie, and these are my brothers, Matthew and Peter. Jonas was just telling us about all that happened after Jesus was crucified."

"Please go on, Jonas. I would love to hear what you have to tell," Cleopas said.

"All right, then," Jonas said, and he and Cleopas sat down on the stone bench while the children settled on the ground at their feet.

"You were telling us about the women," Katie reminded him.

"Ah, yes, the women. Early in the morning on the first day of the week, some of the women who were close to Jesus came to prepare His body with spices and perfumes. But when they arrived, they discovered the tomb was empty. And sitting at the place where the head and the feet of the body had been, were two glorious angels."

"Right here, in this very tomb?" Matthew was awestruck.

"Yes, Matthew," Jonas said, "right here. The angels told the women that Jesus was not here, for He had risen. They instructed the women to go and tell the disciples that Jesus had gone before them into Galilee and that they should go and find Him there. The women were obedient, and they hurried away to find the apostles."

"And what about the guards? What did they do?" Katie wanted to know.

"Oh, they were long gone," Jonas chortled. "When they recovered from fainting, they were so afraid that they ran right out of the garden, even though they weren't supposed to leave their post."

"They were scaredy cats!" Peter declared. "I wouldn't run away like that!"

Katie smiled at him. "Maybe you would if an angel had opened the tomb you were trying to protect."

Peter jumped to his feet and with a swagger pulled an imaginary sword from the sash around his waist. "On guard!" he cried. "I would have used my sword!"

Matthew rolled his eyes. "Do you really think that a sword could hurt an angel of God?" he asked, a little annoyed.

Peter stopped. "Oh, I guess not," he said sheepishly and then sat down again.

Katie turned back to Jonas, "What about the women? What happened to them after the garden?" Katie prompted, eager to hear more.

"They hurried to tell the apostles, just as the

angels had told them to. But the apostles couldn't really believe it. After all, they had just seen Jesus die a terrible death. And the women were telling them He was alive?

"John got here first, bursting through that gate. He raced right there to the tomb's entrance. Peter came running right behind him, and they both looked in to behold the same thing: All that was in the tomb was the linen cloth that had wrapped Jesus' body and the neatly folded linen napkin for his head."

The children sat silent on the ground, enthralled by the story that was tumbling out of Jonas's mouth.

"Now, Mary Magdalene had followed John and Peter here, and she stayed to mourn after they left. She was here in the garden crying when a man came near and asked her, 'Woman, why weepest thou? Whom seekest thou?'

"And guess what? She thought it was me, the gardener! So she answered, 'Because they have taken away the body of my Lord, and I know not where to find him.'"

Katie sniffled loudly, imagining how Mary

must have felt. The person she loved most in the world had been killed in a horrible, violent way. And in her grief, Mary wanted to tenderly care for His body. But it was missing! Probably the people who wanted Him dead had stolen it away!

"But it was really Jesus who was standing there, wasn't it?" Matthew couldn't contain himself any longer.

"Yes, Matthew. It was Jesus who had spoken to Mary," Jonas replied.

"Why didn't she recognize His voice when He spoke?" Katie stopped crying long enough to wonder.

"I can understand *exactly* how it could happen!" Cleopas interjected. "You don't expect that someone who recently died is going to come stand right next to you and speak!" He sounded as if he knew what he was talking about.

"It sounds as though you have a story to tell, too, Cleopas," Jonas said.

"Indeed," Cleopas nodded. "But finish yours first, Jonas. Please. I can share mine after."

"Fair enough," Jonas agreed, and he continued. "Well, when Mary asked where the body of Jesus was, the man didn't exactly answer the question. Instead, He simply called her by name. 'Mary,' He said, and instantly she knew it was Jesus.

"'Rabboni!' she cried, which means *Beloved Master*. And all of her sadness turned to joy."

Jonas stopped talking and took a long look at the tomb. Just then, the little songbird chirped brightly from the branches above the opening, as if to say, "It is true! It is true!"

Then Cleopas closed his eyes, imagining Mary kneeling in the presence of the Savior. "I see it in my mind's eye," he said softly with his hands clasped to his heart, "and I feel it burn within me."

Chapter Five

Of Guavas and Guards

As the afternoon progressed, the shadows began to lengthen in the garden. Cleopas looked up and noted the position of the sun. "Oh, my. I think it is time for me to start for Emmaus. If I do not leave now, I will be traveling in the dark."

"But your story! We have been waiting to hear it." Matthew was clearly disappointed.

"Perhaps it will have to wait for another day," Cleopas said, standing up from the bench.

"But we are just visitors here! We may never be here again. Please can't you tell it to us?" Peter implored.

"Oh, yes, please," Katie echoed Peter.

Looking down at three pair of pleading eyes, Cleopas sighed and said, "You are right. I did say I would share my story with you. Why don't you walk with me a little way, and I will tell it to you as we go."

Jonas cleared his throat meaningfully, as if to remind Cleopas that he, too, had been promised the story.

"Oh Jonas, I forgot! But I will return to this peaceful place many times in the future, and I can tell you about witnessing the resurrected Lord when I come. How would that be?"

Jonas nodded his head. "This is a good plan," Jonas approved. "Besides, it is not good to travel alone after dark. Robbers, you know."

"Thank you for understanding, Jonas," said Cleopas gratefully. "Come children, let us go."

"Good-bye! Thank you, Jonas!" the children called, waving as they followed Cleopas up a stone stairway and through the garden gate.

Jonas waved back as the little band of travelers disappeared into the busy streets of Jerusalem.

Cleopas walked quickly. It was hard for the

children not to stop and gawk. The narrow streets were abuzz with activity. Merchants stood about, showing their wares. Dried fish, wine, fruits, and flat, round loaves of crusty brown bread were displayed up and down the winding alleyways. Peter, especially, looked longingly at the food, listening to his empty stomach rumble.

After walking for a few minutes, the children could see an arched stone gateway just ahead. It looked as if they were about to leave Jerusalem. But at the last moment, Cleopas turned and said to the children, "We have a good walk ahead of us. Before we leave the city market, would anyone like to eat a guava?"

"Would I!" Peter almost shouted. "I'm starving."

Cleopas laughed at the exuberant boy. "Well, we cannot have that, can we? I would like to buy four ripe guavas," he declared to a merchant woman standing before a low table laden with strange foods.

Suddenly, it occurred to Peter that he had no idea what he had just committed to eat. He elbowed Matthew and whispered, "What's a *guava?*"

"No idea, buddy," Matthew shrugged.

"I just hope it's not dried fish," Peter whispered back, holding his stomach and pantomiming a disgusted gag.

Cleopas paid for his purchase and turned to the children, holding four small, green fruits in his hands. They were shaped like elongated apples, but their skins were bumpy and hardened.

The children accepted the guavas gratefully but stood waiting for Cleopas to eat first, for how did one go about eating a guava? Cleopas lifted the small fruit to his mouth and bit right in, as if it were a pear. "Eat, children," he urged, and soon they were all savoring the aromatic, cream-colored flesh.

They quickly discovered that the fruit was full of small, crunchy seeds, but seeing that Cleopas simply chewed and swallowed, they did the same. The children ate around the guava's hardened core just as they would have eaten a pear at home. But as they stood holding their cores, they saw Cleopas devour the whole of his fruit, core and all!

"When in Rome, do as the Romans do," Katie whispered to her brothers, and she started eating her core, just as Cleopas had.

Peter, who obviously had never heard the saying Katie quoted, looked at her as if she were crazy. "We're not in Rome! We're in Jerusalem, right Matthew?"

"Right," Matthew agreed. "But she's just saying that we ought to eat our cores because that seems to be the custom here."

"Well, why didn't you just say so, Katie?" Peter asked cheerfully, and he quickly put what was left of his guava into his mouth.

Cleopas and the children approached the large archway that marked the city's boundary. Two Roman guards dressed in heavy armor and holding long, pointed spears stood at attention on either side of the gate. Each of them wore a short sword in his leather belt. Cleopas and the children passed quickly under the arch, trying not to arouse the attention of the Romans. Away from the soldiers' gaze, they slowed down a bit.

"Is this your first time in Jerusalem?" Cleopas asked the children.

"Yes, but it's not our first time here in Palestine. We visited the River Jordan where John the Baptist preached and baptized," Matthew began.

"And we've also been to the Sea of Galilee." Peter completed the list.

"Well, now you will be able to say that you have walked the road to Emmaus, as well," Cleopas told them.

"Are you going to tell us about what happened to you on this road?" Katie asked him hopefully.

"Yes," he said, taking a long look down the dirt road that stretched in front of them. "This road is now a very special place to me, and I shall never take one step on it for granted again."

As Cleopas talked, two men, apparently headed for Jerusalem, walked toward the little group of travelers. The men were very large and strong-looking, and their unshaven faces were gruff and threatening. As they passed, one of the men elbowed the other, grunted loudly, and pointed to

Katie's long, blonde ponytail. Katie moved to the other side of Cleopas and tried to disappear, unsettled by the way the two men were looking at her. She was grateful and relieved when they were out of view, for something told her they were up to no good.

Chapter Six

The Road to Emmaus

"All right, children," Cleopas began, "here is my story. Another disciple of Jesus and I were traveling along this road. It was the third day after Jesus was crucified, and as we walked, we were talking of all that had happened in the last few days. We had counted on Jesus to save our people, you see. But instead, the people had crucified Him! And now he was gone." Cleopas sounded heartbroken as he remembered.

"You must have been very sad," Peter said, hanging on every word Cleopas spoke.

"Oh, yes." Cleopas was tearful. "We were so

very sad. And the person who always gave us comfort and hope was dead," he continued. "We could hardly take it in.

"As we were talking, a man came up alongside us and began walking with us. He could see that we were troubled, and He asked us, 'What manner of communications are these that ye have one to another, as ye walk, and are sad?'"

"Didn't he know all the things that had happened in Jerusalem?" Matthew asked.

"And didn't he feel the earthquakes and see the sky turn black when Jesus died?" Katie was curious.

"I asked Him that very thing, children. I said, 'You must be a stranger in Jerusalem if you have not heard about all the things that have happened.' And He said, 'What things?' So I told Him how the chief priests and the Roman rulers had delivered Jesus to be crucified."

Cleopas continued, "We also told Him how the women at the tomb had found angels who said that Jesus was alive. I'm sure we sounded skeptical, for we really didn't believe it ourselves. Jesus was alive? It didn't seem possible!"

"Was the man surprised at your story?" Matthew asked.

"He didn't seem surprised at all. In fact, He rebuked us. He said, 'O fools, and slow of heart to believe all that the prophets have spoken: Ought not Christ to have suffered these things, and to enter into his glory?'"

"What did he mean by that?" Matthew was full of questions.

"Looking back, I see that He was trying to teach us, for then He spoke of all the prophets, beginning with Moses. He showed us how each one had prophesied of Jesus and His mission. We began to see that all of history has pointed to this moment, when Jesus would live and then die. And somehow, His death would bring new life and salvation. We didn't fully understand, but our hearts burned within us, and we began to feel hope again.

"Soon we had reached our village, so we asked the man to stay and eat with us. He blessed the bread, and then He broke it and offered it to us. And in that very moment, we suddenly recognized Him."

"Who was it?" Katie asked, wide-eyed.

"It was Jesus Himself," Cleopas said softly. "It was my risen Lord."

"You couldn't tell it was Him all that time?" asked Peter.

"My heart was full of great feeling as He taught us. It felt almost afire with the truths He spoke. But it was not until He gave us the broken bread that we realized who He was," Cleopas explained.

"What did you say to Him?" Katie wondered.

"And what did He say to you?" Matthew pressed.

"Nothing." Cleopas's reply was simple.

"Nothing?" the three children said together.

"As soon as we saw it was Jesus, He disappeared from our sight," Cleopas told them.

"Where did He go?" Peter was confused.

"I do not know," Cleopas answered. "But He stayed long enough to teach us how He had fulfilled the scriptures by rising in glory from the dead. He stayed long enough for us to see that He lives. My Savior lives!"

Moved by the testimony of Cleopas, the children said nothing for a while, for they, too, felt their hearts burn within.

Finally, Peter broke the silence. "What did you do then, Cleopas?"

"Well, we gathered up our things and ran back to Jerusalem. We wanted to tell the apostles what had happened to us. We looked everywhere before we finally found them in the upper room of a house. They had gathered together secretly, for they were afraid to be discovered by the Jews.

"We told them all that had happened to us on the road and in our house. And then, as we were

speaking, Jesus appeared in the room before us. He looked at us tenderly, and then He spoke. The words were gentle, but they penetrated our hearts to the very core. 'Peace be unto you,' he said."

"Were you afraid?" Matthew asked.

"I wasn't, for I had already seen Him once, and I knew that He had risen. But some of the apostles were frightened, thinking that they were seeing a spirit. But then Jesus spoke again, saying 'Why are ye troubled? and why do thoughts arise in your hearts? Behold my hands and my feet, that it is I myself: handle me, and see; for a spirit hath not flesh and bones, as ye see me have.'"

"And did you touch Him?" Katie asked.

"Yes, we all did," he answered. "We felt the scars from the nails that were placed in His hands and feet when He was crucified. Then we knew that this was the same Jesus who had suffered on the cross and had died. But He had come alive again."

"So you have seen Him twice." Katie's voice was full of longing, for she thought Cleopas was the luckiest man in the world.

"Indeed, I have. And because I have received this blessing, I feel responsible to share my witness with others, just as I am doing now. In fact, while we were in the upper room, Jesus gave us a special charge. He said that just as Heavenly Father had sent Him into the world, He was sending *us* into the world to preach repentance."

"He told you to be missionaries!" Matthew marveled.

"Right," Cleopas agreed. "But He didn't just

give us a job to do. He also gave us a special blessing to help us do it. He said 'Receive ye the Holy Ghost.' That is the Spirit we can feel within to help us when Jesus isn't here in person."

"I know what that feels like," Katie said. "I felt it in the garden this morning, and I felt it during your story just now, Cleopas."

"I felt it, too," Matthew added. "It feels kind of warm right here inside," and he pointed to his chest.

Cleopas smiled. "How right you are, children. On this very road I felt my heart burn within me, too. It comforts me to know that even though He is not here, I can always feel His Spirit."

Cleopas slowed his walk, stopped, and looked at the sun, which was getting lower in the sky. "Children, I think we must part ways here. It is not safe to be on this road after dark. If you turn back now and hurry, you will reach Jerusalem before the sun sets."

At the thought of saying good-bye, the children quickly gathered around Cleopas, pressing close and hugging him with great affection. Then tenderly, Cleopas kissed the cheek of each child in turn. "Farewell, my dear friends. Perhaps we shall meet again."

Matthew, Katie, and Peter watched until he went over a rise in the road and disappeared, then reluctantly turned and started their journey back to Jerusalem, keeping their eyes on the setting sun.

Chapter Seven

Highway Robbery

The three children walked briskly along the dusty road. Peter would run ahead, then wait impatiently, while Katie and Matthew walked side by side, talking about what they had heard.

"Well, Katie, *you* knew Grandpa. Suppose he appeared on this road and walked along with us for a while. Since he died many years ago, and you certainly wouldn't *expect* him to appear, would you know it was him?"

"Maybe not. I probably wouldn't take a very good look, since it would never occur to me that my dead Grandpa had come alive and was standing right next to me, talking!"

"See! I think that's how it was for Cleopas! But he *did* recognize the feeling. That feeling when your heart seems to burn, it's really something special, isn't it?"

"It sure is," Katie agreed. As she spoke to Matthew, they rounded a bend in the road. There, right in front of them, were the two large, ferocious-looking men they had seen earlier. And the largest one was holding Peter, with his hand covering Peter's mouth so he couldn't make a sound! Peter was writhing and squirming, desperate to break free, but the man who had captured him was massive, and it looked as if little Peter didn't stand a chance.

"There they are," growled one of the men. "Give us all your money! Do it fast, and you won't get hurt."

"We . . . we . . . don't have any m-m-money." Matthew's voice trembled with fear as he spoke.

"No money?" snarled the man holding Peter. "NO MONEY!" This time he positively roared.

"Steady, Ashram," said the other. "We can always sell the golden hair. Get out your knife."

The man called Ashram grabbed Katie by the wrist, while he used his other hand to take hold of her thick, blonde ponytail and yank her head around.

Now only Matthew was free, and he knew he had to act fast. The man holding Peter reached for his knife and then stepped toward the one who was holding Katie. It was clear: the man with the knife was going to use it to cut off Katie's ponytail while the man named Ashram held her head in his massive grip.

As the two beastly men neared each other, Matthew ducked and squeezed himself right between them. For a moment, the men looked down at Matthew, thoroughly confused. Why was this brazen boy standing between them? Shouldn't he have been running away as fast as he could go?

Acting fast, Matthew grabbed one of Katie's hands, and then he reached for one of Peter's. If only the three children could connect, they might be transported in an instant back through the painting and into Grandma's safe cottage!

But Peter was thrashing about wildly, and Matthew couldn't get hold of his hand. Katie, seeing the problem, cried out, "Peter! Hold still!" The sound of her voice made the robbers hesitate for just a second, and Matthew lunged for Peter's hand. In that moment, the three children—and the golden hair—disappeared with a POOF! And the two dumbfounded robbers found themselves grappling with only thin air.

In the blink of an eye, the children found themselves nestled in pillows and blankets at Grandma's feet. Now safe in the peaceful cottage, the dazed children breathed deeply, listening to Grandma's soothing voice read on about the scene they had just left. Katie, especially, felt grateful for the narrow escape, as she tossed her head back and forth, savoring each swish of her blonde ponytail.

Smiling with relief, she looked over at her two brothers . . . and her heart stopped. The boys were still wearing their Palestine clothes! Then she looked down at herself. She, too, was wearing robes from 2,000 years ago!

"Matthew," she nudged him softly, whispering so Grandma wouldn't hear.

"Oh!" he gasped, wide-eyed with surprise at her attire.

"Shhh," Katie cautioned, putting her finger to her lips.

Matthew pointed to the blankets between them on the floor. The two children covered themselves quickly, concealing their strange outfits. Then Katie gently wrapped another blanket around Peter, who smiled thankfully at his sister and pulled it over his shoulders, unaware of its real purpose.

"'And thus it behooved Christ to suffer,'" Grandma read on, "'and to rise from the dead the third day.' Well, children, that's what happened in Jerusalem." Grandma looked up at her grandchildren as she finished reading the verse.

"Oh, dear, is it cold in here?" she asked, seeing them snuggled in their blankets. "I was so caught up in the story, I didn't notice. I'll get another log for the fire," and Grandma headed outside to the woodpile.

"What are we going to do?" Matthew asked his siblings in a worried voice.

"We've got to get our own clothes back somehow," answered Katie.

"Our own clothes?" Peter questioned. "Well, what are we wearing now?" And he flung off his blanket, shocked at the sight of the brown tunic still tied around his body.

The children heard rustling at the door, and Katie squealed, "Quick, Peter! Cover up!"

"Here we go," Grandma said cheerily as she entered the cottage and fed the fire. "I want you to

stay nice and warm so that we can finish. There's more to the story, you know."

She sat back down and flipped through her scriptures. "After the events in Jerusalem, Jesus appeared in Galilee. Remember, last time we read about that area," and Grandma pointed to her painting of the Sea of Galilee, now framed and mounted on a nearby wall.

"'After these things,' Grandma began reading, 'Jesus showed himself again to the disciples at the sea of Tiberias.' That's another name for the Sea of Galilee, children." As Grandma read, Matthew looked again at the painting that had taken them to the seaside, where they had witnessed many miracles of Jesus.

"'And there were together Simon Peter, and Thomas . . .' Suddenly, a movement in the painting on the wall caught Matthew's eye. The boats in the harbor were bobbing again! He nudged Katie and pointed. They looked at each other, bewildered and thrilled at the same time. Were they being beckoned to the Galilee again? Then Katie had an amazing realization. "Matthew," she whispered, "maybe this is why we're still in these clothes!"

Standing up, she took him by the hand and motioned for him to grab Peter's hand. Then, without hesitation, she thrust her free hand eagerly into the sandy shore in the painting. The wind began to churn, and the children found themselves soaring through the air once again. Then softly, gently, they alighted together alongside the now-familiar sea.

Chapter Eight

Eyes That See and Hearts That Feel

Peter ran exuberantly along the rocky beach, splashing in the shallow water and waving a stick above his head. Matthew and Katie followed behind, trying to keep up with their energetic little brother. It felt good to be back on the shores of the seemingly endless blue sea. Nothing had changed. The old wooden fishing boats were still at anchor along the beach, the sapphire sky arched overhead, and the hills surrounding the lake were blanketed by vivid spring colors.

Then Peter started heading across the sandy lakeshore, running away from the water. "Peter, where are you going?" Katie called. Her blonde ponytail, for which she was now especially thankful, bounced cheerily behind her as she ran to catch up.

"I'm going to the fishing hut," he hollered, without looking back.

"Hey, wait for me," Matthew called out, excited by the possibility of seeing his friends from their last visit to Galilee.

They made their way through a maze of small

shacks where the local fishermen prepared their catch for market. But when they arrived at the one that belonged to Seth's father, they were disappointed to find no one inside.

"Hello," called an elderly man from a nearby fishing hut. "Can I help you?"

"We were looking for our friends. This is their grandpa's fishing hut. Have you seen them?" Matthew asked hopefully.

"Ah, you must mean Seth and his children.

They are often here, for Seth recently joined his father in the fishing trade. But today they have traveled by boat down to Tiberias. They plan to sell dried fish in the marketplace there."

"Oh, phooey." Katie couldn't hide her disappointment.

"Well, I expect they'll be back tomorrow," the man said brightly. "Why don't you come back then?"

"I don't think we'll be here tomorrow," Katie lamented. "Perhaps you could tell them that we were here."

"Certainly," the man said. "Whom shall I say stopped by?"

"I'm Katie. These are my brothers, Matthew and Peter," she said, pointing to the boys in turn.

"It's nice to meet you," said the friendly man. "My name is Zebedee. Seth and Jesse and Abigail are good friends of mine."

"How is Abigail?" Katie wanted to know about her long-crippled friend who had been healed by the Savior. "Is she still healthy and strong?"

Zebedee's dark eyes lit up. "We cannot keep up

with her! She runs everywhere she goes. It is truly a miracle."

"And Seth?" Matthew asked anxiously. "How is he doing in the fishing business?" He was thinking of Seth's courageous decision to leave the tax-collecting profession.

"Oh, he has taken to it like a fish to water," Zebedee chuckled. "He is very happy."

The winds shifted and the smell of fish filled the children's nostrils. Peter held his nose and surveyed the many racks filled with drying fish and at the many large baskets overflowing with whole fish yet to be cleaned. "Where did all these fish come from, Zebedee?" he asked. "There must be thousands of them!"

"Oh, yes, the fish." Zebedee looked about him, overwhelmed. "I must clean them, salt them, and set them to dry before they decay."

"Do you need some help?" Matthew asked.

"I surely do," Zebedee gratefully replied. "Have you cleaned fish before?"

"No . . ." Katie said hesitantly. Then, under her breath to Matthew, she said, "And I'm not sure I want to."

"I'll tell you what," Zebedee suggested. "Why don't I clean and de-bone the fish, and you children can slice them, roll them in salt, and lay them out to dry? Here, let me show you."

The old man and the three children worked together, and soon they had an efficient rhythm going, steadily filling the racks with clean strips of nicely salted fish.

"This sure is a lot of fish for one man to catch," said Peter with admiration. "Do you usually haul in this many at once?"

"Oh, I didn't catch these, Peter," Zebedee assured him. "This is far more than I have ever caught. My sons brought these fish in. But they claim they had some special help."

"What do you mean?" Matthew asked as he continued cutting the raw fish flesh into long strips with Zebedee's knife.

"I'll tell you the story, but I'm not sure it's true." Zebedee's voice sounded doubtful. "One of Jesus' apostles, a man named Simon Peter, decided to go fishing last night. My two sons, James and John, who are also apostles, went along with him. But they fished all night and caught nothing."

"You call this nothing?" Peter was perplexed.

"Hardly." Zebedee smiled wryly. "They say that when the morning came, a man standing on the shore called to them, 'Children, have ye any meat?' They called back, 'No!' The man replied, 'Cast your nets on the right side and ye shall find.'"

"Hadn't they already tried both sides of the boat?" Matthew wanted to know.

"Of course," Zebedee nodded. "After all, they'd been fishing all night long. But they tried it anyway."

"What happened? Did that man know what he was talking about?" Katie asked.

"Oh, He certainly did," Zebedee nodded vigorously. "As soon as James and John let down their net, it was filled with so many fish they could hardly pull it back in. But they got the whole load, and there was not one single tear in the net!"

"It was Jesus who was on the shore, wasn't it?" Matthew guessed.

"Well, that's what my sons tell me. They even say they went ashore and ate a meal with Him." Zebedee shrugged. "But Jesus died last month in Jerusalem! I was there when they lifted His body from the cross. He was dead, I tell you! How could He now be alive?"

"Well, my grandpa died many years ago. And even though my grandma's never seen him, her heart tells her that he's alive." Peter spoke frankly to Zebedee.

Zebedee shook his head skeptically. "A pair of eyes are more reliable than a heart, I've always said. I'll have to see it for myself before I'll believe that a dead man lives again. Even a man as special as Jesus."

Chapter Nine

Be Not Faithless, But Believing

Before the children could respond, a voice rang out. "Zeb-e-dee! Zebedee! Are you here?" A bearded man was wending his way through the maze of fishing huts.

"Thomas!" Zebedee dropped the fish he was cleaning and hurried toward the voice. When the two men met, they threw wide their arms and embraced warmly.

"Thomas, my friend! Are you well?" Zebedee stepped back and looked at Thomas with great affection.

"Very well," Thomas replied. "Oh, how I've

missed you, Zebedee. I came to help with last night's catch, but I see you have already enlisted some friends."

"Oh, yes, my friends," said Zebedee, realizing that introductions were in order. "This is Matthew, Peter, and Katie. And, children, this is my friend Thomas, one of the apostles of Jesus Christ."

"A real apostle?" Peter was obviously impressed.

"Yes, I am," Thomas said kindly. "And I am pleased to meet two boys named Matthew and Peter. Those are the names of two of my fellow apostles, you know."

Peter and Matthew beamed with delight at the acknowledgement.

"And I see Zebedee has wasted no time in putting you to work," he said, surveying the racks of drying fish.

"They arrived just in time to help me save the catch," Zebedee explained to Thomas and added, "And what a catch it is!"

"Only Jesus could do such a miracle," Thomas marveled. "It was wonderful to be with Him again this morning."

"Here we go again." Zebedee sounded

exasperated. "I know He performed miracles when He was alive. But now He is *dead*. I saw the crucifixion, you know. Not even Jesus could have lived through that."

"He didn't, Zebedee," Thomas spoke earnestly. "Jesus really died. But now He is risen. I have seen Him."

"What did He look like, Thomas?" Katie felt shy, but she couldn't contain her curiosity.

"He looked just like Himself," Thomas said. "Just like when He was here with us."

"You and James and John—you have all seen Him. I wish *I* could," Zebedee lamented. "Then I could know for certain."

"Oh, Zebedee, my dear, dear friend. We are so much alike. I have not told you what happened in the week before I saw the risen Lord for the first time, have I?"

"No, but I bet you felt like I do—full of questions and not sure what to believe!" Zebedee sounded frustrated.

"I did. Let's sit, and I'll tell you everything. Matthew, Katie, Peter, come join us." And they all put down their fish and sat upon some old, decaying stumps set around a fire pit to the side of Zebedee's hut. There, with the shimmering blue expanse of the sea before them, the children looked to Thomas expectantly, already enchanted somehow by the story he was yet to tell.

"After Jesus was crucified, most of the apostles were gathered together in the upper room of a house in Jerusalem."

"Oh, yes," Zebedee nodded. "James and John were with them."

"Right," said Thomas. "And while they were there, Jesus appeared in the midst of them."

"Yeah!" Matthew remembered. "Cleopas told us this story."

"Yes, he was there, too."

"How did you feel when you saw Him, Thomas?" Katie asked. "It must have been wonderful."

"Well, I said that *most* of the apostles were in that upper room. Do you know who wasn't there? It was me," Thomas told them.

"You weren't there?" Katie sounded dismayed.

"No, I wasn't. But some of the disciples found me and told me what had happened."

"You must have been so glad to hear that Jesus was alive again!" Matthew's excitement was genuine.

Thomas bowed his head and shook it slightly. "I wish I could say that I was filled with joy. But I was not."

"Why?" Matthew inquired.

Thomas turned and looked at Zebedee with a kind, but sad, smile. "Because I wanted to witness Him with my own eyes. I told my brethren, 'Except I shall see in his hands the print of the nails, and thrust my hand into his side, I will not believe.'"

"That is exactly what I've said!" Zebedee sounded relieved that his friend shared his skepticism. "It is not possible to believe something is true if you haven't seen it for yourself."

"That is what I thought, too," Thomas told him. "But it was Jesus Himself who taught me differently."

"Really? What did He say?" Zebedee's question was sincere and hopeful.

"Well, eight days later, the apostles were again assembled in a room with the doors shut. This time I was with them. Jesus came into the midst of us and said, 'Peace be unto you.'"

"You finally saw Him?" Peter could hardly contain his excitement.

"Yes," Thomas said quietly. "I saw Him. And He spoke right to me: 'Reach hither thy finger, and behold my hands; and reach hither thy hand, and thrust it into my side: and be not faithless, but believing.'"

"What did you do?" Zebedee asked him.

"I felt the prints of the nails in His hands and felt the wound in His side. Then I fell to my knees and said, 'My Lord and my God,' and I wept at His feet."

"Why did you cry? Weren't you happy?" Peter was puzzled.

"Oh, yes. I was overcome with joy to know that my Lord lives. But I was also sorry that I had not believed. 'Be not faithless, but believing,' Jesus told me. I was ashamed that my faith had faltered."

"So He expects me to believe He is risen, even though I have not seen Him?" Zebedee sounded discouraged.

"Well, He said one more thing to me, Zebedee.

And I think He would say the same to you if He were here right now. He said, 'Thomas, because thou hast seen me, thou hast believed: blessed are they that have not seen, and yet have believed.'"

Zebedee repeated the words softly, and with feeling. "'Blessed are they that have not seen, and yet have believed.' So how do I do that, Thomas? How do I believe if I cannot see?"

"That is the right question, Zebedee. How can we know something that we cannot see? Do you remember what happened to the disciples on the road to Emmaus?" Thomas asked.

Zebedee nodded, and Matthew exclaimed, "Yes! We met Cleopas in Jerusalem."

"And he didn't even recognize Jesus while He was walking along with them!" Peter snickered.

Thomas smiled, "True. He did not know who Jesus was, but he said he felt something in his heart."

"A burning, he felt a burning in his heart," Matthew said thoughtfully.

"And what do you think that burning was?" Thomas asked Matthew.

"When I feel that way it's usually the Holy

Ghost trying to teach me something," Matthew replied with feeling.

"Exactly, Matthew." Thomas smiled his approval. "The Holy Ghost can help us feel Jesus in our hearts, even though we cannot see Him with our eyes. I realize now that my heart was telling me that Jesus is risen. I should have trusted that feeling. That's what Jesus wants us to do. 'Blessed are they that have not seen, and yet have believed.'"

Zebedee hung his head and rested his forehead in his hand. Thomas put his arm around his friend's shoulder, and in a moment, Zebedee raised his head and began humming a lilting tune.

"Why is he humming?" Katie turned to Thomas.

"Oh, children, we are in for a treat. Whenever Zebedee has something important to say, he says it in song. Listen, and I think he will sing to us what he is feeling."

And just as Thomas finished speaking, Zebedee began to sing in a light, lovely tenor:

A burning deep inside me, a flame within my heart,

Doth witness of the living Christ, and
　　truth to me impart.
A chosen few have seen Him and their
　　tears have bathed His feet.
But I, I must believe their words, and
　　let the Spirit teach.
So open wide my heart, dear Lord, thy
　　Spirit to receive,
For though my eyes have seen thee not,
　　yet still I will believe.

As Zebedee sang the last words, "Yet still I will believe," his eyes overflowed, and tears freely coursed down both cheeks.

Then he spoke. "Does not my heart burn within me?" he said, his voice choked with emotion. "Oh, Thomas, I believe. I do believe."

Chapter Ten

Home Again

"Father! And Thomas!" A man in the distance was calling toward the fishing hut as he jumped from a boat and pulled it into the shallow water near the shore. Another man clamored out, too, and helped the first pull the boat to safety. They both waved their greetings as they shouted.

Zebedee lit up. "James! John! You have returned," he exclaimed. He hurried to the water's edge, where he hugged and kissed both of his sons. Then Thomas also joined the happy group, embracing them all in brotherly friendship.

Katie, Matthew, and Peter sat near the hut

watching the reunion at the seaside. "Let's join them," Peter suggested, prepared to take off in his customary gallop.

"Hold on, brother," Katie grabbed his elbow. "Are we planning to stay here forever?"

"No, we're not going to stay forever," Matthew assured her. "Unless, of course, you want to." Now he was teasing.

"I think I've smelled enough raw fish for a long time to come," Katie replied emphatically.

"Me, too!" Peter agreed. "Besides, I want to get home to eat my Easter candy!"

"Oh, crumb! We've got candy to eat," Matthew said in mock disappointment. Then his face got serious as he looked toward Katie. "Actually," he said, "I was thinking that it might be time to go."

"I feel the same," said Katie, sighing. "Well, boys, let's take one last look."

It was a beautiful spring day at the Galilee. A cool breeze blew past the children onto the lake. There was no sign of a storm, and seagulls gracefully swooped and dove above the glistening water.

"This is just how I want to remember it,"

Matthew said, trying to forget his last visit to the Sea of Galilee, when a treacherous squall had nearly drowned him.

"Are you ready?" he asked, offering a hand to each of his siblings.

"Wait! Shouldn't we say good-bye?" Katie said, remembering Zebedee and Thomas.

"We could, but it would certainly complicate matters," answered Matthew, looking toward the men at the shore, two of whom the children hadn't even met. "Let's just leave them guessing this time, shall we?" Now Matthew had a mischievous twinkle in his eye.

"If you say so," Katie giggled, and she took her brother's hand.

"I'm ready, too," Peter declared, linking his hand to his brother's, and . . . whoosh! In the twinkling of an eye, the seascape was only a memory and the children were once again at Grandma's feet, safely snuggled in blankets as Grandma finished reading.

The paintings were still. No birds sang at the Garden Tomb. The Sea of Galilee lay motionless. But in the minds of the children, the scenes were alive and real. Katie even thought she could smell a slight fish odor on her hands.

"Grandma, I used to wonder how you could feel Grandpa near even though he isn't here, but now I think I understand," Matthew said.

"You do? Tell me what you mean," she encouraged him.

"Well, on the road to Emmaus, Jesus walked with two disciples, and they didn't know who He was. But even though they couldn't see Him with their eyes, they still felt a burning in their hearts," he explained.

"Their eyes were 'holden,'" Katie reminded him. "That is how the scriptures say that they couldn't see that it was Jesus, at least at first."

"What does that have to do with Grandpa?" Peter was confused.

"I'm trying to get to that. Let me try to explain it better." Matthew was earnest. "Okay, Grandpa really lived here on earth with Grandma, right?"

"Yeah, that's right," Peter answered.

"Well, Jesus lived here on earth, too. The disciples learned that He was alive again when He walked with them because they felt Him in their

hearts first, before they ever saw Him with their eyes," Matthew continued.

"I think I see now," Katie said, a light going on in her head. "Jesus was trying to teach them to trust the feelings in their hearts, wasn't He?"

"Hey! Just like Thomas." Peter was also beginning to get the picture. "Jesus told Thomas that he should have believed that He was risen even without seeing Him."

"That's what I'm trying to say! Grandma knows that Grandpa is alive because she feels it in her heart. And she has faith that one day she will see him again, even though she can't see him with her eyes right now." Matthew finished and looked to Grandma for approval.

"I'd say you are all a lot smarter than I am," she beamed. "Jesus laid down His life for us so that we can all live together with Him again. All we have to do is repent and follow His commandments."

"That sounds easy, but sometimes it's really hard," Peter sighed.

"Just keep trying and you'll be all right. I'm a lot older than you are, and I still have to keep trying, every day. You keep repenting, and He will make up the rest," she said, patting Peter affectionately on the head.

"Hey, Grandma," Peter said, "are there any leftovers? All that traveling made me really hungry!"

Katie shot him a look. "I think he means that running around looking for eggs made him hungry, Grandma."

Peter saw his mistake at once. He jumped up, and bounded out the door before Grandma could ask any questions. "I see some Easter eggs no one found this morning!" he shouted, disappearing into the bushes to retrieve them. Matthew and Katie followed him into the yard, determined to claim some for themselves.

Grandma stood at the window, delighting in their fun. Suddenly, she wrinkled up her nose and peered around, looking for the source of a strange smell she thought she detected. "I declare, I smell something fishy!"

She picked up a can of air freshening spray, but before she could press the nozzle, the painting of Galilee caught her eye. A flood of memories rushed in, and instead of erasing the smell, Grandma sank deep into her rocking chair, closed her eyes, and began singing softly:

> So open wide my heart, dear Lord,
>   thy Spirit to receive,
> For though my eyes have seen thee not,
>   yet still I will believe.

About the Authors

Alice W. Johnson, a published author and composer, is a featured speaker for youth groups, adult firesides, and women's seminars. A former executive in a worldwide strategy consulting company, and then in a leadership training firm, Alice is now a homemaker living in Eagle, Idaho, with her husband and their four young children.

Allison H. Warner gained her early experience living with her family in countries around the world. Returning to the United States as a young woman, she began her vocation as an actress and writer, developing and performing in such productions as *The Farley Family Reunion.* She and her husband reside in Provo, Utah, where they are raising two active boys.

About the Illustrator

Jerry Harston holds a degree in graphic design and has illustrated more than thirty children's books. He has received many honors for his art, and his clients include numerous Fortune 500 corporations. Jerry and his wife, Libby, live in Sandy, Utah. Their six children and sixteen grandchildren serve as excellent critics for his illustrations.